Guests & Messages

GUEST:

TRAVELED FROM:

MESSAGE:

GUEST:

TRAVELED FROM:

MESSAGE:

GUEST:

TRAVELED FROM:

MESSAGE:

GUEST:

TRAVELED FROM:

MESSAGE:

GUEST:

TRAVELED FROM:

MESSAGE:

GUEST:

TRAVELED FROM:

MESSAGE:

GUEST:

TRAVELED FROM:

MESSAGE:

GUEST:

TRAVELED FROM:

MESSAGE:

GUEST:

TRAVELED FROM:

MESSAGE:

GUEST:

TRAVELED FROM:

MESSAGE:

GUEST:

TRAVELED FROM:

MESSAGE:

GUEST:

TRAVELED FROM:

MESSAGE:

GUEST:

TRAVELED FROM:

MESSAGE:

GUEST:

TRAVELED FROM:

MESSAGE:

GUEST:

TRAVELED FROM:

MESSAGE:

GUEST:

TRAVELED FROM:

MESSAGE:

GUEST:

TRAVELED FROM:

MESSAGE:

GUEST:

TRAVELED FROM:

MESSAGE:

GUEST:

TRAVELED FROM:

MESSAGE:

GUEST:

TRAVELED FROM:

MESSAGE:

GUEST:

TRAVELED FROM:

MESSAGE:

GUEST:

TRAVELED FROM:

MESSAGE:

GUEST:

TRAVELED FROM:

MESSAGE:

GUEST:

TRAVELED FROM:

MESSAGE:

GUEST:

TRAVELED FROM:

MESSAGE:

GUEST:

TRAVELED FROM:

MESSAGE:

GUEST:

TRAVELED FROM:

MESSAGE:

GUEST:

TRAVELED FROM:

MESSAGE:

GUEST:

TRAVELED FROM:

MESSAGE:

GUEST:

TRAVELED FROM:

MESSAGE:

GUEST:

TRAVELED FROM:

MESSAGE:

GUEST:

TRAVELED FROM:

MESSAGE:

GUEST:

TRAVELED FROM:

MESSAGE:

GUEST:

TRAVELED FROM:

MESSAGE:

GUEST:

TRAVELED FROM:

MESSAGE:

GUEST:

TRAVELED FROM:

MESSAGE:

GUEST:

TRAVELED FROM:

MESSAGE:

GUEST:

TRAVELED FROM:

MESSAGE:

GUEST:

TRAVELED FROM:

MESSAGE:

GUEST:

TRAVELED FROM:

MESSAGE:

GUEST:

TRAVELED FROM:

MESSAGE:

GUEST:

TRAVELED FROM:

MESSAGE:

GUEST:

TRAVELED FROM:

MESSAGE:

GUEST:

TRAVELED FROM:

MESSAGE:

GUEST:

TRAVELED FROM:

MESSAGE:

GUEST:

TRAVELED FROM:

MESSAGE:

GUEST:

TRAVELED FROM:

MESSAGE:

GUEST:

TRAVELED FROM:

MESSAGE:

GUEST:

TRAVELED FROM:

MESSAGE:

GUEST:

TRAVELED FROM:

MESSAGE:

GUEST:

TRAVELED FROM:

MESSAGE:

GUEST:

TRAVELED FROM:

MESSAGE:

GUEST:

TRAVELED FROM:

MESSAGE:

GUEST:

TRAVELED FROM:

MESSAGE:

GUEST:

TRAVELED FROM:

MESSAGE:

GUEST:

TRAVELED FROM:

MESSAGE:

GUEST:

TRAVELED FROM:

MESSAGE:

GUEST:

TRAVELED FROM:

MESSAGE:

GUEST:

TRAVELED FROM:

MESSAGE:

GUEST:

TRAVELED FROM:

MESSAGE:

GUEST:

TRAVELED FROM:

MESSAGE:

GUEST:

TRAVELED FROM:

MESSAGE:

GUEST:

TRAVELED FROM:

MESSAGE:

GUEST:

TRAVELED FROM:

MESSAGE:

GUEST:

TRAVELED FROM:

MESSAGE:

GUEST:

TRAVELED FROM:

MESSAGE:

GUEST:

TRAVELED FROM:

MESSAGE:

GUEST:

TRAVELED FROM:

MESSAGE:

GUEST:

TRAVELED FROM:

MESSAGE:

GUEST:

TRAVELED FROM:

MESSAGE:

GUEST:

TRAVELED FROM:

MESSAGE:

GUEST:

TRAVELED FROM:

MESSAGE:

GUEST:

TRAVELED FROM:

MESSAGE:

GUEST:

TRAVELED FROM:

MESSAGE:

GUEST:

TRAVELED FROM:

MESSAGE:

GUEST:

TRAVELED FROM:

MESSAGE:

GUEST:

TRAVELED FROM:

MESSAGE:

GUEST:

TRAVELED FROM:

MESSAGE:

GUEST:

TRAVELED FROM:

MESSAGE:

GUEST:

TRAVELED FROM:

MESSAGE:

GUEST:

TRAVELED FROM:

MESSAGE:

GUEST:

TRAVELED FROM:

MESSAGE:

GUEST:

TRAVELED FROM:

MESSAGE:

GUEST:

TRAVELED FROM:

MESSAGE:

GUEST:

TRAVELED FROM:

MESSAGE:

GUEST:

TRAVELED FROM:

MESSAGE:

GUEST:

TRAVELED FROM:

MESSAGE:

GUEST:

TRAVELED FROM:

MESSAGE:

GUEST:

TRAVELED FROM:

MESSAGE:

GUEST:

TRAVELED FROM:

MESSAGE:

GUEST:

TRAVELED FROM:

MESSAGE:

GUEST:

TRAVELED FROM:

MESSAGE:

GUEST:

TRAVELED FROM:

MESSAGE:

GUEST:

TRAVELED FROM:

MESSAGE:

GUEST:

TRAVELED FROM:

MESSAGE:

GUEST:

TRAVELED FROM:

MESSAGE:

GUEST:

TRAVELED FROM:

MESSAGE:

GUEST:

TRAVELED FROM:

MESSAGE:

GUEST:

TRAVELED FROM:

MESSAGE:

GUEST:

TRAVELED FROM:

MESSAGE:

GUEST:

TRAVELED FROM:

MESSAGE:

GUEST:

TRAVELED FROM:

MESSAGE:

GUEST:

TRAVELED FROM:

MESSAGE:

GUEST:

TRAVELED FROM:

MESSAGE:

GUEST:

TRAVELED FROM:

MESSAGE:

GUEST:

TRAVELED FROM:

MESSAGE:

GUEST:

TRAVELED FROM:

MESSAGE:

GUEST:

TRAVELED FROM:

MESSAGE:

GUEST:

TRAVELED FROM:

MESSAGE:

GUEST:

TRAVELED FROM:

MESSAGE:

GUEST:

TRAVELED FROM:

MESSAGE:

GUEST:

TRAVELED FROM:

MESSAGE:

GUEST:

TRAVELED FROM:

MESSAGE:

GUEST:

TRAVELED FROM:

MESSAGE:

GUEST:

TRAVELED FROM:

MESSAGE:

GUEST:

TRAVELED FROM:

MESSAGE:

GUEST:

TRAVELED FROM:

MESSAGE:

GUEST:

TRAVELED FROM:

MESSAGE:

GUEST:

TRAVELED FROM:

MESSAGE:

GUEST:

TRAVELED FROM:

MESSAGE:

GUEST:

TRAVELED FROM:

MESSAGE:

GUEST:

TRAVELED FROM:

MESSAGE:

GUEST:

TRAVELED FROM:

MESSAGE:

GUEST:

TRAVELED FROM:

MESSAGE:

GUEST:

TRAVELED FROM:

MESSAGE:

GUEST:

TRAVELED FROM:

MESSAGE:

GUEST:

TRAVELED FROM:

MESSAGE:

GUEST:

TRAVELED FROM:

MESSAGE:

GUEST:

TRAVELED FROM:

MESSAGE:

GUEST:

TRAVELED FROM:

MESSAGE:

GUEST:

TRAVELED FROM:

MESSAGE:

GUEST:

TRAVELED FROM:

MESSAGE:

GUEST:

TRAVELED FROM:

MESSAGE:

GUEST:

TRAVELED FROM:

MESSAGE:

GUEST:

TRAVELED FROM:

MESSAGE:

GUEST:

TRAVELED FROM:

MESSAGE:

GUEST:

TRAVELED FROM:

MESSAGE:

GUEST:

TRAVELED FROM:

MESSAGE:

GUEST:

TRAVELED FROM:

MESSAGE:

GUEST:

TRAVELED FROM:

MESSAGE:

GUEST:

TRAVELED FROM:

MESSAGE:

GUEST:

TRAVELED FROM:

MESSAGE:

GUEST:

TRAVELED FROM:

MESSAGE:

GUEST:

TRAVELED FROM:

MESSAGE:

GUEST:

TRAVELED FROM:

MESSAGE:

GUEST:

TRAVELED FROM:

MESSAGE:

GUEST:

TRAVELED FROM:

MESSAGE:

GUEST:

TRAVELED FROM:

MESSAGE:

GUEST:

TRAVELED FROM:

MESSAGE:

GUEST:

TRAVELED FROM:

MESSAGE:

GUEST:

TRAVELED FROM:

MESSAGE:

GUEST:

TRAVELED FROM:

MESSAGE:

GUEST:

TRAVELED FROM:

MESSAGE:

GUEST:

TRAVELED FROM:

MESSAGE:

GUEST:

TRAVELED FROM:

MESSAGE:

GUEST:

TRAVELED FROM:

MESSAGE:

GUEST:

TRAVELED FROM:

MESSAGE:

GUEST:

TRAVELED FROM:

MESSAGE:

GUEST:

TRAVELED FROM:

MESSAGE:

GUEST:

TRAVELED FROM:

MESSAGE:

GUEST:

TRAVELED FROM:

MESSAGE:

GUEST:

TRAVELED FROM:

MESSAGE:

GUEST:

TRAVELED FROM:

MESSAGE:

GUEST:

TRAVELED FROM:

MESSAGE:

GUEST:

TRAVELED FROM:

MESSAGE:

GUEST:

TRAVELED FROM:

MESSAGE:

GUEST:

TRAVELED FROM:

MESSAGE:

GUEST:

TRAVELED FROM:

MESSAGE:

GUEST:

TRAVELED FROM:

MESSAGE:

GUEST:

TRAVELED FROM:

MESSAGE:

GUEST:

TRAVELED FROM:

MESSAGE:

GUEST:

TRAVELED FROM:

MESSAGE:

GUEST:

TRAVELED FROM:

MESSAGE:

GUEST:

TRAVELED FROM:

MESSAGE:

GUEST:

TRAVELED FROM:

MESSAGE:

GUEST:

TRAVELED FROM:

MESSAGE:

GUEST:

TRAVELED FROM:

MESSAGE:

GUEST:

TRAVELED FROM:

MESSAGE:

GUEST:

TRAVELED FROM:

MESSAGE:

GUEST:

TRAVELED FROM:

MESSAGE:

GUEST:

TRAVELED FROM:

MESSAGE:

GUEST:

TRAVELED FROM:

MESSAGE:

GUEST:

TRAVELED FROM:

MESSAGE:

GUEST:

TRAVELED FROM:

MESSAGE:

GUEST:

TRAVELED FROM:

MESSAGE:

GUEST:

TRAVELED FROM:

MESSAGE:

GUEST:

TRAVELED FROM:

MESSAGE:

GUEST:

TRAVELED FROM:

MESSAGE:

GUEST:

TRAVELED FROM:

MESSAGE:

GUEST:

TRAVELED FROM:

MESSAGE:

GUEST:

TRAVELED FROM:

MESSAGE:

GUEST:

TRAVELED FROM:

MESSAGE:

GUEST:

TRAVELED FROM:

MESSAGE:

GUEST:

TRAVELED FROM:

MESSAGE:

GUEST:

TRAVELED FROM:

MESSAGE:

GUEST:

TRAVELED FROM:

MESSAGE:

GUEST:

TRAVELED FROM:

MESSAGE:

GUEST:

TRAVELED FROM:

MESSAGE:

GUEST:

TRAVELED FROM:

MESSAGE:

GUEST:

TRAVELED FROM:

MESSAGE:

GUEST:

TRAVELED FROM:

MESSAGE:

GUEST:

TRAVELED FROM:

MESSAGE:

GUEST:

TRAVELED FROM:

MESSAGE:

GUEST:

TRAVELED FROM:

MESSAGE:

GUEST:

TRAVELED FROM:

MESSAGE:

GUEST:

TRAVELED FROM:

MESSAGE:

GUEST:

TRAVELED FROM:

MESSAGE:

GUEST:

TRAVELED FROM:

MESSAGE:

GUEST:

TRAVELED FROM:

MESSAGE:

GUEST:

TRAVELED FROM:

MESSAGE:

GUEST:

TRAVELED FROM:

MESSAGE:

GUEST:

TRAVELED FROM:

MESSAGE:

GUEST:

TRAVELED FROM:

MESSAGE:

GUEST:

TRAVELED FROM:

MESSAGE:

GUEST:

TRAVELED FROM:

MESSAGE:

GUEST:

TRAVELED FROM:

MESSAGE:

GUEST:

TRAVELED FROM:

MESSAGE:

GUEST:

TRAVELED FROM:

MESSAGE:

GUEST:

TRAVELED FROM:

MESSAGE:

GUEST:

TRAVELED FROM:

MESSAGE:

GUEST:

TRAVELED FROM:

MESSAGE:

GUEST:

TRAVELED FROM:

MESSAGE:

GUEST:

TRAVELED FROM:

MESSAGE:

GUEST:

TRAVELED FROM:

MESSAGE:

GUEST:

TRAVELED FROM:

MESSAGE:

GUEST:

TRAVELED FROM:

MESSAGE:

GUEST:

TRAVELED FROM:

MESSAGE:

GUEST:

TRAVELED FROM:

MESSAGE:

GUEST:

TRAVELED FROM:

MESSAGE:

GUEST:

TRAVELED FROM:

MESSAGE:

GUEST:

TRAVELED FROM:

MESSAGE:

GUEST:

TRAVELED FROM:

MESSAGE:

GUEST:

TRAVELED FROM:

MESSAGE:

GUEST:

TRAVELED FROM:

MESSAGE:

GUEST:

TRAVELED FROM:

MESSAGE:

GUEST:

TRAVELED FROM:

MESSAGE:

GUEST:

TRAVELED FROM:

MESSAGE:

GUEST:

TRAVELED FROM:

MESSAGE:

GUEST:

TRAVELED FROM:

MESSAGE:

GUEST:

TRAVELED FROM:

MESSAGE:

GUEST:

TRAVELED FROM:

MESSAGE:

GUEST:

TRAVELED FROM:

MESSAGE:

GUEST:

TRAVELED FROM:

MESSAGE:

GUEST:

TRAVELED FROM:

MESSAGE:

GUEST:

TRAVELED FROM:

MESSAGE:

GUEST:

TRAVELED FROM:

MESSAGE:

GUEST:

TRAVELED FROM:

MESSAGE:

GUEST:

TRAVELED FROM:

MESSAGE:

GUEST:

TRAVELED FROM:

MESSAGE:

GUEST:

TRAVELED FROM:

MESSAGE:

GUEST:

TRAVELED FROM:

MESSAGE:

GUEST:

TRAVELED FROM:

MESSAGE:

GUEST:

TRAVELED FROM:

MESSAGE:

GUEST:

TRAVELED FROM:

MESSAGE:

GUEST:

TRAVELED FROM:

MESSAGE:

GUEST:

TRAVELED FROM:

MESSAGE:

GUEST:

TRAVELED FROM:

MESSAGE:

GUEST:

TRAVELED FROM:

MESSAGE:

GUEST:

TRAVELED FROM:

MESSAGE:

GUEST:

TRAVELED FROM:

MESSAGE:

GUEST:

TRAVELED FROM:

MESSAGE:

GUEST:

TRAVELED FROM:

MESSAGE:

GUEST:

TRAVELED FROM:

MESSAGE:

GUEST:

TRAVELED FROM:

MESSAGE:

GUEST:

TRAVELED FROM:

MESSAGE:

GUEST:

TRAVELED FROM:

MESSAGE:

GUEST:

TRAVELED FROM:

MESSAGE:

GUEST:

TRAVELED FROM:

MESSAGE:

GUEST:

TRAVELED FROM:

MESSAGE:

GUEST:

TRAVELED FROM:

MESSAGE:

GUEST:

TRAVELED FROM:

MESSAGE:

GUEST:

TRAVELED FROM:

MESSAGE:

GUEST:

TRAVELED FROM:

MESSAGE:

GUEST:

TRAVELED FROM:

MESSAGE:

GUEST:

TRAVELED FROM:

MESSAGE:

GUEST:

TRAVELED FROM:

MESSAGE:

GUEST:

TRAVELED FROM:

MESSAGE:

GUEST:

TRAVELED FROM:

MESSAGE:

GUEST:

TRAVELED FROM:

MESSAGE:

GUEST:

TRAVELED FROM:

MESSAGE:

GUEST:

TRAVELED FROM:

MESSAGE:

GUEST:

TRAVELED FROM:

MESSAGE:

GUEST:

TRAVELED FROM:

MESSAGE:

GUEST:

TRAVELED FROM:

MESSAGE:

GUEST:

TRAVELED FROM:

MESSAGE:

GUEST:

TRAVELED FROM:

MESSAGE:

GUEST:

TRAVELED FROM:

MESSAGE:

GUEST:

TRAVELED FROM:

MESSAGE:

GUEST:

TRAVELED FROM:

MESSAGE:

GUEST:

TRAVELED FROM:

MESSAGE:

GUEST:

TRAVELED FROM:

MESSAGE:

GUEST:

TRAVELED FROM:

MESSAGE:

GUEST:

TRAVELED FROM:

MESSAGE:

GUEST:

TRAVELED FROM:

MESSAGE:

Made in the USA
Columbia, SC
06 September 2022

66712925R00057